olive oil

by Tess Mallos

TUTTLE PUBLISHING
Tokyo • Rutland, Vermont • Singapore

Published by Tuttle Publishing, an imprint of Periplus
Editions, with editorial offices at 130 Joo Seng Road,
#06-01, Singapore 368357, and 364 Innovation Drive,
North Clarendon, VT 05759, USA.

Hardcover ISBN 13: 978-0-8048-3919-8
          ISBN 10: 0-8048-3919-0
Printed in Malaysia

Distributed by
North America, Latin America and Europe
Tuttle Publishing, 364 Innovation Drive,
North Clarendon, VT 05759-9436.
Tel: (802) 773-8930 Fax: (802) 773-6993
Email: info@tuttlepublishing.com
www.tuttlepublishing.com

Asia Pacific
Berkeley Books Pte Ltd.
130 Joo Seng Road #06-01
Singapore 368357.
Tel: (65) 6280-1330 Fax: (65) 6280-6290
Email: inquiries@periplus.com.sg
www.periplus.com

10 09 08 07
5 4 3 2 1

Contents

Introducing Olive Oil 6

Essential Ingredients Used in This
   Book 8

All About Oilve Oil 10

Basics and Sauces 12

Appetizers 19

Salads 38

Soups 48

Vegetables 54

Pasta 62

Poultry 68

Seafood 74

Meat 88

Complete List of Recipes 96

Introducing Olive Oil

It is believed that the cultivation of the olive tree began in the Eastern Mediterranean some 6000 years ago. The oil was used for lighting, and in perfumed unguents and cleansers for the body, as well as for cooking. The Minoans traded olive oil from Crete in about 2000 BCE, with subsequent Greek and Phoenician seafarers continuing the trade, carrying it as far west as Spain and today's Morocco. From 750 BCE the Greeks planted olive trees in their colonies in eastern Spain, southern France, Italy and Sicily; where the Greeks did not plant them, the Carthaginians and the Romans did.

Today, the principal world olive oil producer is Spain, followed by Italy, Greece, Tunisia, Turkey, Syria, Morocco and Algeria. However, olive oil is increasingly being produced outside the Mediterranean, in places such as Australia, Africa and California. Each country's oil has a distinctive flavor.

Olive oil, the world's most commonly eaten mono-unsaturated oil, has been enjoyed for many thousands of years around the Mediterranean. Not only does it taste good, but there is a mass of evidence that a diet based on olive oil can promote longer life and may prevent some of the diseases associated with our usual western eating pattern. In recent years, medical researchers have turned their attention to the virtues of the Mediterranean style of eating and to olive oil. On closer inspection, this ancient oil has proved to be more than just a source of mono-unsaturated fat. It is also a rich source of antioxidants—substances now attracting great scientific attention.

Olive oil contains a wide variety of valuable antioxidants that are not found in other oils. Epidemiological studies suggest that olive oil has a protective effect against certain malignant tumors in the breast, prostate, endometrium and digestive tract. Research has revealed that the "type" rather than the "quantity" of fat seems to have more implications for cancer incidence. This could be related to oleic acid, which is the predominant mono-unsaturated fatty acid in olive oil.

It has been demonstrated that the addition of olive oil to a diet that is not changed in any other way has a lowering effect on blood pressure. A diet rich in olive oil is not only a good alternative in the treatment of diabetes; it may also help to prevent or delay the onset of the disease by preventing insulin resistance and its possible harmful implications by raising HDL cholesterol, lowering triglycerides, and ensuring better blood sugar level control and lower blood pressure.

Like all other fats and oils, olive oil is high in calories, which could suggest that it would contribute to obesity. However, evidence shows that there is less obesity amongst Mediterranean people, who consume the most olive oil in the world. It has been demonstrated that a diet rich in olive oil leads to greater and longer-lasting weight loss than a low-fat diet. Olive oil tastes good and it is a stimulus to eat vegetables and pulses. Olive oil bolsters the immune system against external attacks from micro-organisms, bacteria or viruses. The fatty acids in olive oil are good allies in lowering important immunological parameters.

Olive oil is also good for the stomach, hepato-bilary system, pancreas and intestines. It helps with osteoporosis, cognitive function and skin damage. It is also beneficial to consume olive oil during pregnancy and whilst breast feeding.

Essential Ingredients Used in This Book

Chili peppers come in many varieties. The recipes in this book generally call for fresh finger-length Asian chilies with medium heat. If you prefer less heat, remove the seeds and white membranes of the chilies before using them in the dish.

Coriander is the most widely used herb in Asian cuisines. The whole plant is used—the roots, stems and leaves. The seeds are roasted and then ground and used in curry pastes. **Coriander roots** are ground into spice pastes, while **coriander leaves** (cilantro) are more often used as a garnish. For storage, wash and dry the fresh leaves before placing

them in a plastic bag in the refrigerator—they will keep for 5-6 day. Italian parsley or basil may be substituted, although the flavor is not exactly the same.

Cumin seeds are from a plant in the parsley family. Briefly dry-roasting the seeds brings out their flavor, which is earthy, pungent and a little bitter. Used whole or ground, cumin seeds are a common ingredient in spice mixes, curries and raitas. Black cumin seeds have a slightly less bitter flavor.

Eggplant, also known as aubergine, is a spongy, mild-tasting vegetable. Eggplants come in many shapes, sizes and colors. The recipes in this book call for globe or American eggplants, which are large, dark purple and

pear-shaped. Do not use the long and slender Japanese or Chinese varieties. Pick egg-plants that are firm, with smooth, shiny skins and bright green stems.

Octopus, except baby octo-pus, needs to be tenderized before using: Clean it thoroughly and discard the head. Remove the little hard ball (or "beak") in the center and cut off the last $3/4$ in (2 cm) of the tentacles. Rinse well with cold water and drain. Half-fill a pot, large enough to accommodate the octopus, with water and bring it to a boil. Quickly immerse the octopus completely in the boiling water for about 3 seconds, then remove it. Return the water to a boil and repeat the process 2 more times. Bring a fresh pot of water to a boil and add 1 halved onion and 1 bay leaf. Then add the octopus and simmer gently until it is tender. This may take $1/2$ to 3 hours, depending on the thickness of the tentacles. After about 30 minutes of cooking, cut out a small piece of the octopus and bite into it to test for tenderness; repeat every 15 minutes or so until the octopus is tender. Remove the cooked octopus from the pot and drain, then cut the tentacles into bite-size cross-sections.

Paprika is made from red peppers that are dried and ground to produce a powder that is used to flavor and add color to savory dishes. Paprika is available in various heat levels; mild forms, with the flavor of bell pepper (capsicum) are used in this book.

Peppercorns are "the king of spices" and feature extensively in Indian cooking. Both ground black and white peppercorns are used in this book. Always grind peppercorns just before adding to a dish to ensure the best aroma and flavor.

Soy sauce   Dark soy sauce   Sweet black sauce

Soy sauce is brewed from soybeans and wheat fermented with salt. It is a clear brown liquid with a salty taste and is used as a table condiment and cooking seasoning. **Dark soy sauce** is denser and less salty, with a malty tang. **Sweet black soy sauce** is a thick, fragrant sauce used in marinades and sauces. It is not widely available in the West but can be approximated by adding $1/2$ teaspoon of dark brown sugar to 1 tablespoon of normal dark soy sauce. Hoisin sauce also makes a good substitute.

Squids are best used fresh. You have to clean them yourself, but the reward is an infinitely better flavor. To clean a squid, pull out its head and attached intestines from the tubelike body. Remove and discard the long, thin cartilage. Cut off the wings if desired and remove and discard the eyes and beak from the mouth. Peel the outer skin off the body with your fingers, and use the body tube and tentacles as directed in the recipes after rinsing them under cold running water.

Saffron threads are the dried stigmas from a variety of crocus flowers, each of which produces only three stigmas. Harvesting saffron is labor-intensive, making it the most costly spice in the world. Saffron threads are generally soaked in a warm liquid to release their intense gold-yellow color and pungent, earthy aroma and flavor.

All About Olive Oil

Types of Olive Oil

Extra virgin and virgin olive oils are from the first pressing, and have a fruity flavor and a greenish tinge which fades to a clear golden color. They have a long shelf life as they are low in oleic-free fatty acid. High in antioxidants, they remain stable after repeated use in deep-frying. However, they lose their fruity flavor when subjected to high temperatures. Some extra virgin and virgin oils, having undergone minimal processing, may solidify when refrigerated. This does not affect the flavor of the oil, and once brought to room temperature it will revert to a liquid. As these oils are more expensive, use them with discretion.

Olive oil is a blend of refined olive oil with some virgin oil added to restore the distinctive flavor and color. It is the most widely used oil and is suitable for deep-frying; it can be reused a number of times, providing it is strained through a double layer of muslin into a clean container and stored in a cool place between uses.

Light and extra light olive oil is 100 per cent olive oil, but refined and blended with just enough virgin oil to given them a light, subtle taste. This oil is excellent when you do not want to mask the flavor of the other ingredients. Although not widely available, they are also worthwhile seeking out if you have had an aversion to the taste of olive oil in the past, but wish to use it for its health benefits.

Choosing an Olive Oil

This is very much a matter of taste. Some extra virgin olive oils from Italy, particularly Tuscany, are prized for their peppery bite, which may be a little strong for some palates. Olive oils from Greece are renowned for their excellent flavor and quality, particularly those from the Peloponnese and Crete regions. Other extra virgin olive oils have distinctive fruity flavors. Buy a small bottle first, before investing in a larger bottle or can.

Is color important? The color of olive oil depends on the pigments in the fruit. Green olives, harvested early in the season, give a green oil because of their high chlorophyll content. Ripe olives, harvested later in the season, give a yellow oil because of the carotenoid (yellow-red) pigments. The color of the oil is influenced by the exact combination and proportions of pigments.

How long does olive oil last? Olive oil does not improve with age like wine. A peppery oil will sometimes mellow a little, but olive oil can oxidize and become rancid under the best storage conditions in a few years. Air, light and heat are its enemies. Store your oil in dark containers, in a cool cupboard. Rancidity is the most common fault in olive oil. It causes the oil to smell like "stale walnuts" and have an off taste with little or no fruit flavor.

Classic Oil and Lemon Dressing

$1/2$ cup (125 ml) olive oil
3 tablespoons freshly-squeezed
    lemon juice
2 tablespoons chopped fresh
    oregano or parsley (optional)
$1/2$ teaspoon salt, or to taste
Freshly-ground black pepper, to
    taste

Combine all the ingredients in a bowl and beat well with a fork until blended. As the oil and lemon juice will separate on standing, beat the dressing again just before using. Serve well with fried fish and on salads. May also be used to brush on fish and shellfish when grilling.

Makes about $3/4$ cup (150 ml)

Classic Oil and Vinegar Dressing

$1/2$ cup (125 ml) olive oil
2 tablespoons wine vinegar
$1/2$ teaspoon dried mustard
2 tablespoons chopped fresh
    oregano or parsley (optional)
$1/2$ teaspoon salt
Freshly-ground black pepper, to
    taste

Combine all the ingredients in a bowl and beat well with a fork until blended. As the oil and lemon juice will separate on standing, beat the dressing again just before using. Serve well with raw vegetable salads.

Makes about $3/4$ cup (150 ml)

Basic Italian Dressing

$3/4$ cup (200 ml) olive oil
3 tablespoons red or white wine
    vinegar
2 teaspoons freshly-squeezed
    lemon juice
1 teaspoon dried oregano, or 2
    tablespoons minced fresh basil
    or parsley
2 teaspoons minced garlic
$1/2$ teaspoon onion powder
$1/2$ teaspoon garlic powder
$1/2$ teaspoon paparika
Sugar, salt and freshly-ground
    black pepper, to taste

Combine all the ingredients in a jar, close tightly and shake until well blended. As the oil and lemon juice will separate on standing, shake the dressing again just before using. Serve well with raw vegetable salads.

Makes about 1 cup (250 ml)

Homemade Pesto Sauce

2 cups (80 g) fresh basil leaves
$1/_2$ cup (50 g) pine nuts
3 cloves garlic, peeled
1 cup (250 ml) virgin olive oil
$1/_2$ cup (60 g) freshly-grated
  parmesan cheese
$1/_4$ cup (30 g) freshly-grated
  pecorino cheese
Salt and freshly-ground black
  pepper, to taste
Olive oil, for storing

Makes about 2 cups (500 ml)

1 Rinse the basil leaves well, discarding any damaged ones. Dry the leaves in a salad spinner, or by spreading them on paper towels or a cloth for 1 hour.

2 Dry-roast the pine nuts in a dry skillet over low heat for about 5 minutes until light brown, stirring often. Remove from the heat and cool. Combine with the basil leaves and garlic, and process to a coarse purée in a food processor, adding a little olive oil to facilitate processing. Add the cheeses and continue processing to a smooth paste. With the motor running, gradually pour in the remaining olive oil. Season with the salt and pepper.

3 To store, transfer the pesto to a sterilized jar, cover with a thin layer of olive oil, seal and refrigerate for up to 4 days.

Note: The Ligurians insist that their famous basil sauce can only be made in a marble mortar with a wooden pestle—it is the crushing action that gives the pesto its name. I prefer to use a food processor to make this sauce as it takes but a minute or two. Do not use a blender, though, as you may lose the special texture. The quantity of sauce given is generous, because it has other uses besides serving on pasta—in Liguria, the favored pasta is trenette (thin ribbon pasta). Use with boiled potatoes, or spoon over fish or potato gnocchi.

Classic Italian Tomato Sauce

Two 15-oz (425-g) cans tomatoes,
   chopped but undrained
2 onions, quartered
2 bay leaves
2 cloves garlic, peeled
3 tablespoons olive oil
1 teaspoon sugar
Salt and freshly-ground black
   pepper, to taste
$1/4$ cup (5 g) fresh Italian parsley
2 tablespoons fresh basil leaves

Makes about 4 cups (1 liter)

1 Combine all the ingredients, except the herbs, in a saucepan and bring to a boil. Reduce the heat to a gentle simmer, cover and cook for 40 minutes. Add the herbs and simmer for a further 15 minutes. Remove from the heat, then process in a blender or food processor until smooth. Alternatively, pass through a food mill fitted with a medium screen set over a bowl.
2 If using the sauce immediately, return to the pan and bring to a boil again. To store, pour into warmed sterilized jars, cool and seal with sterilized plastic lids. Refrigerate for up to 2 weeks.

Note: This is an easy version of tomato sauce for any pasta and for use in other recipes. It is convenient to have it on hand for quick-to-prepare meals. Canned tomatoes, preferably Italian, should be used—they have a better flavor than fresh tomatoes, particularly in winter, when tomatoes are not at their sun-ripened best.

Spanish Tomato Sauce

3 tablespoons olive oil
2 large onions, quartered
2 cloves garlic, peeled
2 red bell peppers, cored,
   deseeded and chopped
One 15-oz (425-g) can tomatoes,
   chopped but undrained
3 tablespoons fresh parsley
1 tablespoon fresh thyme
Salt and freshly-ground black
   pepper, to taste
2 tablespoons fino (dry) sherry

Makes about 4 cups (1 liter)

1 Warm the olive oil in a saucepan over low heat. Add the onion and cook, stirring from time to time, for 5–10 minutes, until transparent. Add the garlic and sauté for 1 minute, then add the pepper, cover and cook for 15 minutes.
2 Add all the other ingredients except the sherry, cover and cook for about 20 minutes, until thick. Remove from the heat, then process to a purée with a hand-held blender, or in a food processor.
3 Return the purée to the pan, add the sherry and warm through over low heat, adjusting the seasoning. Remove from the heat. Use immediately or transfer to a sealed, sterilized jar and store in the refrigerator for up to 2 weeks.

Note: Tomato sauces can vary greatly, according to their regions and uses. This is a Spanish version that can be served with barbecued meat or over pasta or rice.

Homemade Mayonnaise

3 egg yolks
1 teaspoon salt
$1/2$ teaspoon mustard powder
1 tablespoon freshly-squeezed
   lemon juice or white wine vinegar
1 cup (250 ml) olive oil
Freshly-ground white pepper,
   to taste
1 tablespoon lukewarm water

Makes about 2 cups (500 ml)

Process the egg yolks, salt, mustard and $1/2$ of the lemon juice or vinegar in a food processor until pale. With the motor running, gradually add the olive oil—begin by pouring in a thin stream and then in a steady stream when the mayonnaise starts to thicken. Stop processing as soon as all the oil has added. Add the ground pepper and remaining lemon juice or vinegar, then pour in the water and process briefly. Transfer to a bowl, cover and refrigerate until required, or transfer to a sealed sterilized jar and keep for up to 1 month.

Note: Extra virgin olive oil is not suitable for this recipe as the flavor is too strong. Mayonnaise should not be left at room temperature for more than 4 hours, or it will turn bad. The lukewarm water stops the mayonnaise from separating under refrigeration.

Variation: For Aioli (Garlic Mayonnaise), omit the mustard, use 2 tablespoons of lemon juice or vinegar and add 4–6 cloves of crushed garlic before processing,

Olive Tapenade

1$^1/_2$ cups (300 g) pitted black
  olives, rinsed well
2 tablespoons chopped canned
  anchovy fillets
3 tablespoons drained capers
1 clove garlic, chopped
2 teaspoons red wine vinegar
Salt and freshly-ground black
  pepper, to taste
$^1/_4$ cup (60 ml) olive oil

Makes about 1$^1/_2$ cups (375 ml)

Process all the ingredients, except the olive oil to a
coarse purée in a food processor, then with the motor
running, gradually pour in the olive oil in a thin stream.
Transfer to a bowl, cover and refrigerate until required.
Bring to room temperature before serving.

Note: Tapenade can be served in a small pot as an
accompaniment to crudités (raw vegetable pieces), or
used as a spread on slices of toasted or fresh baguette.
It is available commercially but is easy to make with a
food processor and keeps for weeks in the refrigerator
—pack into small, sterilized jars, cover with a thin layer
of olive oil and seal with sterilized plastic lids.

Marinated Olives

Adding flavorings to olives makes them even more appealing as appetizers. While many are available already marinated, it is easy to make your own. These are some of the ways in which cured olives are prepared in the Mediterranean. For all olives, rinse and drain well before using.

Spain

1 lb (500 g) pitted olives
3 cloves garlic, halved
1 teaspoon ground cumin
1 teaspoon each chopped fresh
  thyme, marjoram and rosemary
$1/2$ teaspoon fennel seeds
2 bay leaves, crumbled
$1/4$ cup (60 ml) sherry vinegar
$1/4$ cup (60 ml) olive oil

Combine all the ingredients in a large bowl and mix well. Transfer to a jar, seal and allow to stand at room temperature for 2 days before using, shaking occasionally to distribute the marinade. The olives can be stored in the refrigerator for up to 1 week. Bring to the room temperature before serving.

Makes about 3 cups

Cyprus

1 lb (500 g) pitted green olives
1 tablespoon coarsely-crushed
 coriander seeds
2 cloves garlic, crushed
Freshly-squeezed juice of 1 lemon
$1/4$ cup (60 ml) olive oil

Crack the olives by hitting them sharply with the flat of a cleaver or meat mallet. Combine with all the other ingredients in a bowl. Mix well and marinate for 2 hours. Store in a sealed jar in the refrigerator for up to 2 weeks. Bring to the room temperature before serving.

Makes about $2^1/2$ cups

Italy

1 lb (500 g) pitted black olives
 (the shrivelled variety is excellent)
2–3 cloves garlic, halved
Olive oil, to store

Place the olives and garlic in a jar and cover with olive oil. Seal and allow to stand at room temperature for 2–3 days. Serve immediately or refrigerate for up to 2 weeks.

Makes about $2^1/2$ cups

Tunisia

1 lb (500 g) pitted olives
2 teaspoons harissa
$1/2$ cup (125 ml) olive oil

Makes about $2^1/2$ cups

Combine all the ingredients and mix well. Transfer to a sealed jar and refrigerate for 1–2 days before using. Bring to the room temperature before serving. Olives can be stored in the refrigerator for up to 1 month—shake the jar occasionally to distribute the marinade.

Morocco

1 lb (500 g) pitted olives
2 tablespoons finely-chopped
 fresh Italian parsley
2 tablespoons finely-chopped
 fresh coriander leaves (cilantro)
2 cloves garlic, finely chopped
1 tablespoon finely-chopped
 preserved lemon peel (page 42)
1 teaspoon finely-chopped red
 finger-length chili pepper
$1/2$ teaspoon ground cumin
2 tablespoons fresh lemon juice
$1/2$ cup (125 ml) olive oil

Combine all the ingredients in a bowl and mix well. Transfer to a jar, seal and refrigerate for 1–2 days. Bring to the room temperature before serving.

Note: You can use 2 teaspoons of freshly-grated orange rind and 3 tablespoons of freshly-squeezed lemon juice in place of the preserved lemon peel.

Makes about $3^1/2$ cups

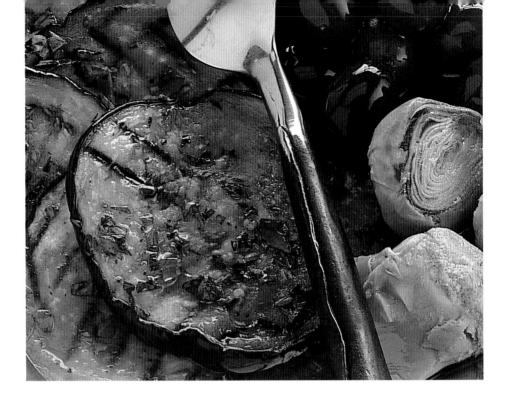

Marinated Eggplant

2 lbs (1 kg) eggplants, stems
  removed
Salt, to taste
Olive oil

Marinade
$1/_2$ cup (125 ml) extra virgin
  olive oil
2 tablespoons red wine or balsamic
  vinegar
2 cloves garlic, finely chopped
2 tablespoons finely-chopped
  fresh basil leaves
Freshly-ground black pepper, to
  taste

Serves 6

1 Slice the eggplants into $1/_4$-in (5-mm) thick slices.
Place in a colander, sprinkling each layer with salt. Set
aside for 30 minutes, then rinse and press dry in paper
towels or a clean cloth.
2 Preheat a broiler (grill) until very hot. Place a layer of
the eggplant slices on a lightly greased baking pan and
brush with olive oil. In batches, cook under the broiler
(grill) for 5–10 minutes, turning to brown evenly.
Remove from the heat and transfer the cooked eggplant
slices to a shallow dish. Alternatively, fry the eggplant
slices in olive oil until golden and tender.
3 Combine the Marinade ingredients in a bowl and
mix well, then pour over the cooked eggplant and
refrigerate for 2–3 hours or overnight. Serve at room
temperature as an antipasto.

Roasted Bell Peppers

6 bell peppers
3–4 cloves garlic, thinly sliced
Salt and freshly-ground black
 pepper, to taste
$^1/_2$ cup (125 ml) extra virgin
 olive oil

Serves 6–8

1 Preheat the oven to 425–450 °F (220–230 °C).
2 Cut the bell peppers in half through the stem and place, cut-side down, in a baking sheet lined with foil. Bake or broil the pepper halves for about 15 minutes, or until the skins are blistered and charred.
3 Place the blistered pepper halves in a plastic bag, seal and allow to stand for 15 minutes to steam. Remove the pepper from the bag, peel away and discard the skins. Remove the core, seeds and white membranes.
4 Slice the pepper halves into wide strips and place in a shallow dish. Sprinkle with the garlic slices, salt and black pepper to taste, then cover with the olive oil. Serve immediately or cover and refrigerate until required. Bring to the room temperature before serving as an antipasto.

Note: Use a fruity virgin olive oil. Some oils solidify when chilled; once brought to the room temperature, they will revert to a liquid.

Bruschetta with Arugula

$^1/_2$ cup (125 ml) extra virgin
  olive oil
2 cloves garlic, halved
12 thick slices Italian bread
6–8 ripe tomatoes, deseeded and
  cut into thin wedges
Salt and freshly-ground black
  pepper, to taste
3 tablespoons chopped sun-dried
  tomatoes (optional)
1 cup (30 g) small fresh arugula
  leaves, rinsed and dried well

Serves 4–6

1 Combine the olive oil and garlic in a jug, then allow to stand for 30 minutes.
2 Toast the bread slices over moderate heat under a broiler (grill) until golden on both sides.
3 To serve, overlap the tomato wedges on each bruschetta and season with the salt and pepper. Sprinkle lightly with the chopped sun-dried tomato (if using) and top each with 3–4 arugula leaves. Slightly overlap the bruschetta on serving platters and garnish with the remaining arugula leaves. Strain the olive oil with garlic over the bruschetta and serve immediately.

Deep-fried Calamari Rings

2 lbs (1 kg) fresh squids (calamari)

Oil, for deep-frying

$1/_2$ cup (60 g) all-purpose (plain) flour, for dredging

2 eggs, beaten with 1 tablespoon water

$1^1/_2$ cups (90 g) breadcrumbs, to coat the squids

Garlic Dipping Sauce

3 cloves garlic, peeled

1 potato, peeled and blanched until soft, then mashed with a fork

1 slice white bread

$1/_3$ cup (100 ml) olive oil

1 tablespoon freshly-squeezed lemon juice

1 tablespoon white wine vinegar

Salt and freshly-ground white pepper, to taste

1 Prepare the Garlic Dipping Sauce first by pulsing all the ingredients in a food processor until light and smooth. This takes only a few seconds. Do not process for too long; the mixture can heat up, causing the oil to separate. Transfer to a bowl, cover and chill in the refrigerator until ready to use.

2 Clean the squids thoroughly, discarding the heads but retaining the tentacles. Remove the beak in the center of the tentacles. Slice each tube into rings and rinse well.

3 Half-fill a heavy-bottomed saucepan with oil and heat to 350–400 °F (180–200 °C). Working in batches, dredge the squid with the flour, then dip into the egg mixture and roll in the breadcrumbs until well coated. Gently lower the coated squid into the hot oil and deep-fry until golden brown on all sides, about 1 minute. Remove and drain on paper towels. Serve immediately with a dipping bowl of Garlic Dipping Sauce on the side.

Serves 4–6

Onion and Olive Tart

One 6-oz (170-g) can anchovy
  fillets, drained and halved
  lengthwise (optional)
8–10 pitted black olives, halved
1 tablespoon extra virgin olive oil

Pastry
2 cups (250 g) all-purpose (plain)
  flour, sifted
$3/4$ cup (170 g) chopped butter
1 egg yolk
2–3 tablespoons iced water

Topping
2 lb (1 kg) onions, thinly sliced
$1/4$ cup (60 ml) olive oil
1 bay leaf, halved
3 cloves garlic, finely chopped
2 teaspoons chopped fresh thyme
1 teaspoon chopped fresh rosemary
Salt and freshly-ground black
  pepper

Serves 6

1 Make the Pastry by processing the flour and butter
in a mixer until the mixture resembles coarse breadcrumbs. Add the egg yolk and 1 tablespoon of the
iced water and process very briefly, just until the dough
gathers on the blades—adding the remaining water if
necessary. Remove from the mixer and refrigerate the
dough, wrapped in plastic wrap, for 30 minutes.
2 To make the Topping, combine the onion slices, oil
and bay leaf in a wide saucepan. Cover and cook over
low heat for 20–30 minutes, stirring occasionally, until
the onion is soft but not browned. Add all the other
ingredients and cook uncovered over a slightly
increased heat for about 10 minutes, until the moisture
has evaporated. Remove from the heat, discard the
bay leaf and allow to cool.
3 Preheat the oven to 400 °F (200 °C).
4 On a lightly floured surface, roll out the Pastry dough
to a rectangle 11 x 13 in (28 x 33 cm). Lift onto a 10 x
12-in (25 x 30-cm) Swiss roll tin, molding it into the
shape and crimping the edges if desire. Prick the
dough well with a fork and bake in the oven for 15
minutes. Remove the Pastry from the oven and reduce
the heat to 350 °F (180 °C).
5 Spread the cooled Topping over the pastry crust,
and top with the anchovy fillets (if using) and olive
halves in a lattice pattern (as shown in the photo), if
desired. Brush with the olive oil and return to bake for
25 minutes until cooked. Serve hot.

Turkish Pita Bread

2$^1/_2$ teaspoons (7 g) active dry yeast

$^1/_2$ teaspoon sugar

1$^1/_2$ cups (375 ml) lukewarm water

4 cups (500 g) strong bread flour or all-purpose (plain) flour

1 teaspoon salt

$^1/_4$ cup (60 ml) olive oil

1 tablespoon toasted sesame seeds or nigella (black cumin seeds)

Makes 3 loaves

1 In a small bowl, mix the yeast and sugar with $^1/_2$ cup (125 ml) of the warm water.

2 Sift the flour and salt into a mixing bowl. Make a well in the center and pour in the yeast mixture and remaining warm water. Stir a little of the flour into the yeast mixture, cover and allow to stand for 10 minutes in a warm place until frothy.

3 Add the olive oil to the flour mixture and mix into a soft dough, adding a little extra water if the dough is too firm. Turn the dough out onto a lightly floured work surface and knead by hand until smooth and elastic, about 10 minutes. Only add extra flour if the dough remains sticky after a few minutes of kneading. Shape the dough into a ball, cover with a kitchen towel, and allow to rise at room temperature until doubled in volume.

4 Punch down the dough, then knead for a couple of minutes. Divide into 3 equal portions and shape each into an oval loaf about 8 in (20 cm) long. Holding your thumb and two fingers together, make 4 deep spaced out depressions along the center of each loaf. Cover with a kitchen towel and allow to rest for 15–20 minutes.

5 Preheat the oven to 450 °F (230 °C), with a large baking pan placed on the center shelf of the oven.

6 Brush the loaves lightly with water and sprinkle with the sesame seeds or nigella. Pick up one loaf by sliding your hands underneath, then lift and gently pull out to stretch to about 10–12 in (25–30 cm) long. Place the stretched loaf into the hot baking pan in the oven, leaving room for other loaves, and close the oven door immediately to retain heat. Repeat to stretch the remaining loaves. Bake the loaves until lightly browned and sound hollow when tapped, 8–10 minutes. Remove from the heat, cool on a wire rack and use on the day of baking, or wrap well and freeze. Serve with dips and main meals.

Note: If your baking sheet is of normal size, bake one loaf at a time, removing bread and returning baking sheet to oven to reheat before cooking the next loaf.

Homemade Anchovy Paste

One 2-oz (60g) can or jar anchovy
  fillets in olive oil, drained
Fresh milk, enough to cover
$1/2$ cup (125 ml) extra virgin
  olive oil
2 cloves garlic, chopped
2 teaspoons chopped fresh thyme
  or winter savory
1 tablespoon red wine vinegar
Freshly-ground black pepper,
  to taste
1 loaf French country-style bread,
  sliced
Radishes, chicory spears, black
  olives, to serve

1 Place the anchovy fillets in a bowl and pour in
enough milk to cover. Allow to soak for 2 minutes to
reduce the saltiness. Drain and rinse the fillets well and
pat dry with paper towels.
2 Process the anchovy fillets with the olive oil, garlic,
thyme and vinegar to a smooth purée in a food
processor, then season with the black pepper to taste.
Transfer to a serving bowl.
3 To serve in the traditional way, toast the bread on
one side under a hot broiler (grill) until golden, spread
the untoasted side with the anchovy paste and continue
broiling until the anchovy paste is bubbling. Serve with
radishes, chicory spears and olives.

Makes about $3/4$ cup (200 ml)

Herbal Toasts with Bean Dip

2 cloves garlic, chopped
1 small red onion, chopped
Half a 15-oz (425-g) can white
  kidney beans, drained and rinsed
2 tablespoons chopped parsley
1 tablespoon olive oil
Freshly-squeezed juice of $1/2$ lemon
Salt and freshly-ground black
  pepper, to taste
1 teaspoon extra virgin olive oil,
  to serve

Bread Toasts
$1/2$–1 loaf focaccia bread, sliced
Olive oil, for brushing
$1/2$ cup (20 g) chopped fresh
  herbs of choice (rosemary,
  thyme, Italian parsley and dill)
Salt, to taste

1 Process the garlic, onion and beans in a food processor
until smooth, then add the parsley, oil and lemon juice
and process until well combined, about 10 seconds.
Season with the salt and pepper. Transfer to a serving
bowl, cover and refrigerate until ready to serve. Just
before serving, drizzle with the extra virgin olive oil.
2 To make the Bread Toasts, preheat the oven to 400 °F
(200 °C). Brush one side of each bread slice with olive
oil, top generously with the herbs and sprinkle with
the salt. Bake in the oven until golden and crisp, about
7 minutes. Serve hot or at room temperature with the
bean dip.

Serves 6–8

Baked Ricotta Cheese with Olives and Sundried Tomatoes

1 lb (500 g) fresh ricotta cheese
  block or wedge
3 tablespoons olive oil
Freshly-ground black pepper,
  to taste
Paprika, to taste
$1/2$ portion Homemade Pesto
  Sauce (page 14)
Crusty Italian bread or focaccia,
  to serve

Accompaniments
Sun-dried tomatoes
Sun-dried red peppers
Olives
Sliced cucumber

Serves 8–10

1 Preheat the oven to 350 °F (180 °C).
2 Prepare the Homemade Pesto Sauce following the recipe on page 14.
3 Pat dry the ricotta cheese very gently with paper towels. Pour $1/2$ of the olive oil into a casserole dish and add the ricotta. Sprinkle the top with black pepper to taste and a light dusting of paprika, and drizzle over the remaining olive oil. Cover and bake for 10 minutes, basting once with the oil in the casserole dish. Remove the lid and bake for a further 10 minutes, basting with the oil in the same manner. If the cheese has not browned, place it under a hot broiler (grill) for 3–4 minutes. Remove from the heat.
4 Place the ricotta on one side of large serving platters and arrange the Accompaniments on the other side. Serve hot or at room temperature with crusty bread or focaccia, and a serving bowl of Homemade Pesto Sauce on the side. To store, cover and refrigerate until required.

Garlic Mushrooms

1 lb (500 g) mixed fresh mushrooms
5 tablespoons olive oil
3 cloves garlic, thinly sliced
1 tablespoon freshly-squeezed
lemon juice
Salt and freshly-ground black pepper, to taste
3 tablespoons finely-chopped
fresh parsley

Serves 4–6

1 Wash the mushrooms only if they are wild. Otherwise,
wipe over the mushrooms with a slightly moistened
cloth. Trim the stems and leave the mushrooms whole;
if they are large, slice thickly.
2 Heat the oil in a large skillet and sauté the mushrooms
and garlic over high heat for 3–5 minutes, until lightly
browned. Stir often and do not allow the garlic to
burn. Season with the lemon juice, salt and pepper to
taste. Remove from the heat, transfer to a warmed
dish and sprinkle with the chopped parsley. Serve hot
or at room temperature.

Stuffed Red Peppers

2 large red bell peppers
2 tablespoons sour cream, to
serve

Filling
1 tablespoon olive oil
1 medium onion, sliced
1 clove garlic, minced
$1^{1}/_{2}$ cups (150 g) chopped eggplant
2 tablespoons chopped fresh
Italian parsley
$^{1}/_{4}$ cup (15 g) chopped canned
capers, or chopped green olives
6 canned anchovy fillets,
chopped
2 ripe tomatoes, chopped
4 tablespoons grated parmesan
$^{1}/_{2}$ cup (50 g) cooked brown rice

1 Cut the bell peppers in half lengthwise, removing the
seeds and membranes. Place the bell pepper halves on
a baking pan.
2 Preheat the oven to 350 °F (180 °C)
3 To prepare the Filling, heat the oil in a large skillet and
sauté the onion and garlic over medium heat for 1–2
minutes, until fragrant and soft. Stir in the chopped
eggplant, parsley, caper, anchovy and tomato, and
continue to sauté for about 3 minutes. Add the cheese
and rice, and mix well. Remove from the heat and cool.
4 Fill the bell pepper halves with the Filling and bake in
the oven for about 4 minutes until tender and cooked.
Remove from the heat and serve immediately with small
dollops of sour cream.

Serves 4

Tomato and Olive Salad

4 firm ripe tomatoes

2 young cucumbers, thinly sliced

$1/4$ cup (60 ml) freshly-squeezed lemon juice

1 tablespoon white vinegar

$1/4$ cup (60 ml) olive oil

1 teaspoon finely-chopped fresh mint

1 tablespoon finely-chopped fresh Italian parsley

Salt and freshly-ground black pepper, to taste

One 2-oz (60-g) can pitted black olives, drained

Parsley sprigs, to garnish

1 Peel the tomatoes if desired. Thinly slice the tomatoes and arrange on an oval platter, overlapping one another slightly, then lay the cucumber slices on top of the tomato slices on one side.

2 Combine the lemon juice, vinegar, olive oil, herbs, salt and pepper in a bowl and mix well, adjusting the taste. Pour the dressing over the tomato and cucumber slices. Cover and refrigerate until ready to serve.

3 Just before serving, arrange the olives on the other side of the tomato slices and garnish the platter with parsley sprigs.

Note: This salad accompanies most Turkish meals, particularly in summer when tomatoes are at their best.

Serves 4

Cherry Tomato, Bocconcini and Basil Skewers

24 cherry tomatoes

Salt and freshly-ground black pepper, to taste

24 baby bocconcini

24 small fresh basil leaves

24 short bamboo skewers

Extra virgin olive oil, to serve

Cut each cherry tomato in half lengthwise and season with the salt and pepper. To assemble, thread a tomato half on a skewer, followed by a bocconcini, a basil leaf and another tomato half. Repeat with the remaining ingredients and skewers. Serve immediately with a dipping bowl of olive oil on the side.

Makes 24 skewers

Roasted Tomato and Bell Pepper Salad

6 large, firm ripe tomatoes
2 green and 2 red bell peppers
2 small onions, whole and unpeeled
2 red or green finger-length chili
  peppers
4 tablespoons olive oil
2 cloves garlic, crushed
Salt and freshly-ground white
  pepper, to taste
1 tablespoon finely-chopped
  Italian parsley
Pitted black olives, to serve

Serves 6

1 Preheat the oven to 425–450°F (220–230°C).
2 Place the tomatoes, bell peppers and onions in a baking pan and roast for 15 minutes, then turn, add the chili peppers and roast for 15 minutes more. Remove from the oven.
3 Place the bell peppers in a plastic bag, seal and allow to stand for 15 minutes to steam. Peel the tomatoes and cut into small pieces, draining the juice and discarding the loose seeds. Halve the chili peppers, deseed and scrape the flesh from the skin. Peel and slice the onions. When the peppers are steamed, peel, halve and deseed, discarding the membranes, then dice.
4 Beat the chili pulp, oil and garlic in a large bowl. Add the roasted vegetables, and salt and pepper to taste, then mix lightly. Cool to room temperature. Transfer to a shallow serving dish, sprinkle with the parsley and scatter the olives over the top.

Orange and Olive Salad

4 sweet oranges
1 red onion, sliced into rings
$3/4$ cup (150 g) pitted black
  olives, rinsed and drained
$1/4$ cup (60 ml) olive oil
Pinch of cayenne pepper
1 teaspoon superfine (castor)
  sugar
Coriander leaves (cilantro), to
  garnish

Serves 4

1 Peel the oranges using a serrated knife, removing all traces of white pith and outer membranes. Slice into $1/4$-in (5-mm) slices on a plate to gather the juices. Arrange the orange slices on a shallow serving platter. Scatter the onion rings and olives over the orange slices.
2 Pour the orange juice into a small bowl. Add the olive oil, cayenne pepper and sugar, and beat well until the sugar is dissolved, then pour over the salad and toss to combine. Garnish with the coriander leaves (cilantro) and serve immediately.

Tomato, Onion and Lemon Salad

2 lb (1 kg) firm ripe tomatoes,
  peeled and deseeded, then
  diced
1 red onion, sliced into rings
$1/_2$ preserved lemon (see note)

Dressing
$1/_3$ cup (100 ml) olive oil
1 tablespoon freshly-squeezed
  lemon juice
1 clove garlic, crushed
2 tablespoons chopped fresh
  Italian parsley
2 tablespoons chopped fresh
  coriander leaves (cilantro)
$1/_4$ teaspoon ground cumin
$1/_4$ teaspoon paprika
Salt and freshly-ground black
  pepper, to taste

Serves 6

1 Combine the tomato dice and onion rings in a bowl. Discard the pulp from the preserved lemon and rinse the peel well. Dry with paper towels and sliced into fine strips crosswise. Add to the bowl of tomato and onion.
2 To prepare the Dressing, beat all the ingredients in a bowl until well combined. Pour the Dressing over the tomato and onion mixture and toss lightly. Cover and allow the salad to stand for 30 minutes. Serve at room temperature.

Note: To preserve lemons, set aside $1/_3$ cup (80 g) rock salt. Cut 2 washed lemons into quarters from stem end, leaving them joined at the base. Sprinkle the cut surfaces with salt and press back into shape. Halve and juice 3–4 lemons and cut the skins in half. Place 1 tablespoon of the salt into a sterilized 2-cups (500-ml) jar. Add 1 lemon, fill the spaces with 2–3 pieces of peel and repeat, sprinkling with the salt. Half-fill the jar with the lemon juice and top with cooled, boiled water. Top with the lemon peel and seal tightly. Store in cool dark cupboard, tilting occasionally, for 4 weeks.

Borlotti Bean and Radicchio Salad

1 lb (500 g) shelled dried borlotti
(cranberry) beans, rinsed
Salt
2 heads radicchio (red chicory),
leaves separated
1 small onion, sliced
$1/2$ cup (125 ml) extra virgin
olive oil
2 tablespoons red wine vinegar
Freshly-ground black pepper, to
taste

Serves 6

1 Place the beans in a saucepan and cover generously with water. Bring slowly to a boil and simmer over low heat, uncovered, until tender, 15–20 minutes. Remove from the heat and drain. Add $3/4$ teaspoon of salt to the cooked beans and toss well. Allow to cool until warm.
2 Wash and dry the radicchio leaves in a salad spinner or by wrapping them in paper towels or a clean cloth. Reserve a few larger outer leaves and slice the remaining leaves into $1/4$ in (5 mm) wide strips. Combine with the onion and warm beans in a large bowl.
3 In a small bowl, beat the olive oil with the vinegar, and season with the salt and pepper to taste. Pour over the salad and toss well.
4 Line a shallow serving dish with the reserved radicchio leaves, pile the salad on top and serve immediately.

Beet Salad with Oranges and Walnuts

6 medium beets (beetroots)
Salt, to taste
2 sweet oranges
3 tablespoons olive oil
1 tablespoon red wine vinegar
Freshly-ground black pepper, to
taste
8–10 romaine (cos) lettuce leaves,
torn into pieces
$1/2$ cup (60 g) walnut pieces, dry-
roasted over low heat, then
broken into smaller pieces.

Serves 6

1 Cut the tops off the beets and discard. Rinse the beets well, place in a saucepan with water to cover and season with a little salt. Bring to a boil and simmer over low heat until tender, 40–50 minutes. Remove from the heat, drain and cool. Peel and cut each beet into half and then slice into wedges. Place the beet wedges in a bowl.
2 Peel the oranges using a serrated knife, removing all traces of white pith and outer membranes. Segment by cutting between visible membranes, catching the juice in a bowl. Squeeze the remains of the oranges into the bowl and reserve the juice. Set the orange segments aside separately.
3 In a bowl, beat the orange juice with the olive oil, vinegar, salt and pepper to taste, then pour $1/2$ of the mixture over the beet wedges and toss lightly.
4 Place the lettuce leaf pieces in a large, shallow serving bowl, add the remaining dressing and toss well. Top with the beet wedges and orange segments, and sprinkled with the walnut. Serve immediately.

Orange and Carrot Salad

Moroccan orange salads are refreshing and palate-cleansing. They go well with meat and poultry dishes, although Morocco salads are served as an appetizer and left on the table to be picked at during the remainder of the meal.

3 sweet oranges
2 medium carrots, cut into thin shreds
Freshly-squeezed orange juice
2 tablespoons freshly-squeezed lemon juice
1 tablespoon superfine (castor) sugar
2 tablespoons olive oil
Salt and freshly-ground black pepper, to taste
1 tablespoon orange flower water
Ground cinnamon, for dusting
Sprigs of coriander leaves (cilantro) or Italian parsley, to garnish

Serves 6

1 Peel the oranges using a serrated knife, removing all traces of white pith and outer membranes. Segment by cutting between visible membranes, catching the juice in a bowl. Squeeze the remains of the oranges into the bowl and reserve the juice. Place $3/_4$ of the orange segments in a bowl with the carrot shreds and set aside the remaining orange segments.

2 Top up the reserved orange juice with freshly-squeezed orange juice to make $1/_4$ cup (60 ml), then combine with the lemon juice and sugar in a small bowl, and stir until the sugar is dissolved. Beat in the olive oil and salt and pepper to taste, then pour over the salad and toss until well combined. Cover the salad and refrigerate until ready to serve, along with the reserved orange segments.

3 To serve, transfer to a shallow platter and stir in the reserved orange segments. Sprinkle with the orange flower water and dust lightly with the cinnamon, then garnish with the coriander or parsley sprigs.

Variation: To make Orange and Radish Salad, replace the carrots with 10 round, red radishes sliced very thinly. Toss as instructed and place in a shallow bowl lined with romaine (cos) lettuce leaves.

Gazpacho

2 lb (1 kg) ripe tomatoes, peel and
  deseed
2 medium sweet long green peppers or bell peppers, halved and
  deseed
2 small cucumbers, peeled
1 medium onion, peeled
1 clove garlic, chopped
1 cup (60g) soft white breadcrumbs
2 tablespoons red wine vinegar
4 tablespoons olive oil
$1/_2$ teaspoon ground cumin
  (optional)
$1/_4$ teaspoon cayenne pepper
Salt, to taste
3 cups (750 ml) iced water
Tomato juice (optional)

Garlic Croûtons
3 thick slices stale white bread
6 tablespoons olive oil
1 clove garlic, halved

Serves 6

1 Set aside 1 tomato, 1 pepper, 1 small cucumber and
$1/_2$ an onion. Roughly chop the remaining vegetables
and process to a purée with the garlic in a food processor. Add the breadcrumbs, vinegar and oil and pulse
briefly. Add the ground cumin (if using) and season
with the cayenne pepper and salt to taste. Transfer to a
bowl, cover and refrigerate for at least 2 hours.
2 Dice the reserved vegetables and refrigerate covered
until ready to serve.
3 To make the Garlic Croûtons, remove the crusts from
the bread slices and cut the bread into $1/_2$-in (1-cm)
cubes. Heat the olive oil and garlic in a skillet until hot,
then remove the garlic. Add the bread cubes and fry
until golden and crisp, stirring often. Remove from the
heat and drain on paper towels.
4 To serve, pour the purée into a large glass or pottery
bowl and stir in the iced water, or a combination of
water and tomato juice if the tomatoes used were not
fully flavored, and garnish with a small amount of the
diced vegetables. Serve with bowls of the remaining
diced vegetables and the Garlic Croûtons.

Garlic Almond Soup

1 cup (150 g) whole blanched
  almonds
$^1/_2$ cup (50 g) pine nuts
3 cloves garlic, peeled
$^3/_4$ cup (45 g) soft white breadcrumbs
3 cups (750 ml) iced water
$^1/_4$ cup (60 ml) olive oil
2–3 tablespoons sherry vinegar
Salt, to taste
$1^1/_2$ cups (180 g) seedless grapes,
  to serve

Serves 6

1 Process the almonds, pine nuts and garlic in a food processor until roughly chopped—do not overprocess or the nuts will become oily. Add the breadcrumbs and $^1/_2$ cup (125 ml) of the iced water and process to a smooth purée, scraping down the sides of the bowl occasionally. With the motor running, gradually pour in the olive oil.

2 Transfer to a large bowl and mix in the remaining iced water. Season with the sherry vinegar and salt to taste, cover and refrigerate until ready to serve.

3 Check the consistency before serving—if it is too thick, add a little more iced water. Serve in a soup tureen, in a large glass bowl, or in individual serving bowls, with floating grapes on the surface.

Broccoli Soup with Potato

$1^1/_2$ lbs (750 g) broccoli
2 potatoes, peeled and chopped
$^1/_2$ cup (125 ml) olive oil
5 cloves garlic, peeled
1 small onion, peeled
2 teaspoons chopped fresh thyme
6 cups (1 liters) chicken or
  vegetable stock
2 tablespoon freshly-squeezed
  lemon juice
Salt and freshly-ground black
  pepper, to taste
Toasted bread slices and cheese,
  to serve

Serves 6

1 Cut off the stems and roughly chop the broccoli. Peel and thinly slice the stems. In a pot, bring to a boil with all the other ingredients except the salt and pepper, then simmer over low heat, covered, for 4–5 hours. Remove from the heat.

2 In batches, process the broccoli mixture to a purée in a food processor. Season with salt and pepper to taste and ladle into individual serving bowls. Serve with toasted bread slices and cheese.

Chickpea Soup with Linguine

1 cup (200 g) dried garbanzo
  beans (chickpeas)
6 cups (1$^1/_2$ liters) water
1 large sprig fresh rosemary
$^1/_3$ cup (100 ml) olive oil
1 medium onion, sliced
2 cloves garlic, chopped
2 tablespoons tomato paste
Salt and freshly-ground black
  pepper, to taste
5 oz (150 g) dried linguine,
  broken into short lengths
1 tablespoon chopped fresh
  rosemary (optional)
Crusty bread, to serve
Extra virgin olive oil, to serve

Serves 6

1 Rinse the beans well, place in a saucepan with 3 cups (750 ml) of the water and soak overnight in the refrigerator.

2 Add the remaining water and rosemary sprig to the the saucepan and bring the bean mixture to a boil. Cover and simmer over low heat until tender, about 1$^1/_2$ hours. Remove from the heat and discard the rosemary sprig.

3 Heat the oil in a skillet and sauté the onion over medium heat until transparent, 1–2 minutes. Add the garlic and sauté for 30 seconds. Stir in the tomato paste and 1 cup (250 ml) of the cooked bean liquid. Remove from the heat and pour into the saucepan with the cooked beans.

4 Season the bean mixture with salt and pepper to taste, and bring to a boil over medium heat. Stir in the pasta and simmer gently until the pasta is tender, about 10 minutes. Remove from the heat, transfer to individual serving bowls and garnish with the chopped rosemary, if using. Serve hot with crusty bread and a small jug of olive oil.

Stuffed Tomatoes

12 ripe medium tomatoes

Sugar, to taste

Salt and freshly-ground black
  pepper, to taste

$1/2$ cup (125 ml) olive oil

1 onion, diced

1 clove garlic, finely chopped

4 tablespoons pine nuts (optional)

1 cup (200 g) uncooked long-grain
  rice, washed

3 tablespoons chopped fresh basil

$1^1/2$ cups (375 ml) water

2 tablespoons tomato paste

Serves 4–6

1 Slice the tops off the tomatoes and reserve for use as the lids. Scoop out the pulp with a melon baller or a teaspoon and reserve. Sprinkle the cavities with sugar and set aside.

2 In a saucepan, combine the reserved tomato pulp with salt and pepper to taste and $1/2$ teaspoon of sugar, and cook over medium-low heat until soft, stirring. Remove from the heat and press through a sieve into a bowl. Set aside.

3 Heat $1/2$ of the olive oil in a skillet and sauté the onion and garlic over medium heat until tender, 1–2 minutes. Add the pine nuts (if using) and cook for a further 2 minutes. Stir in the tomato pulp, rice, $1/2$ of the basil and 1 cup (250 ml) of the water. Cover and simmer over low heat for about 10 minutes, until the rice is half-cooked and the liquid is absorbed. Remove from the heat and season with salt and pepper to taste.

4 Preheat the oven to 325 °F (160 °C).

5 Spoon the mixture loosely into the tomatoes and put on the tops. Pour a little oil in a baking pan, arrange the tomatoes in the pan and spoon over the remaining olive oil. Combine the tomato paste with 1 teaspoon of sugar, the remaining water, and salt and pepper to taste, mix well and pour around the stuffed tomatoes in the pan. Bake uncovered for 30–35 minutes, until the rice is cooked. Serve hot or at room temperature.

Stuffed Vine Leaves

28–48 fresh or preserved vine
  leaves
$1/4$ cup (60 ml) olive oil
2 cups (500 ml) water
1 lemon, thinly sliced
Yogurt, to serve

Rice Filling
$1/2$ cup (125 ml) olive oil
2 large onions, finely chopped
1 cup (200 g) uncooked short-
  grain rice, washed
4 tablespoons pine nuts
4 tablespoons currants
1 teaspoon ground allspice
2 tablespoons finely-chopped
  fresh dill
Salt and freshly-ground black
  pepper, to taste

Makes 20–40 parcels

1 Bring a pot of water to a boil and blanch the vine leaves, in batches, for about 2 minutes until soft. Remove from the heat, dip in cold water to cool and then drain well. Set aside.

2 To prepare the Rice Filling, heat the olive oil in a skillet and sauté the onion over medium heat until transparent, 2–3 minutes. Add the rice and cook, stirring, for 2 minutes. Stir in the pine nuts, currants, allspice, dill, and season with salt and pepper to taste. Cover and cook over low heat for 5 minutes. Remove from the heat and set aside.

3 To make the parcels, place 1 vine leaf, shiny-side down, on a working surface and spoon 1–2 tablespoons of the Rice Filling (depending on the size of the leaf) to the center. Fold the stem end of the leaf over the Filling, tuck in the sides and brush the leaf with the olive oil, then roll up tightly into a neat parcel. Reserving 8 vine leaves, continue to make the parcels with the remaining ingredients.

4 Line the base of a large heavy-based saucepan with 4 vine leaves, then arrange the parcels, folded-side down and closely packed, on top of the leaves in a single layer. As each layer is completed, top with 3 lemon slices before beginning the next layer. When all the parcels have been placed in the pan, top with 3 lemon slices and cover with the remaining vine leaves. Pour the olive oil and water over the parcels, and place a heavy plate on top, inverted, to keep the parcels in shape during cooking.

5 Bring the parcels to a slow simmer, then reduce the heat to low, cover and continue to simmer gently for 50 minutes. Remove from the heat and allow to cool. Serve chilled or at room temperature with a bowl of yogurt on the side.

Mixed Vegetable Ratatouille

8 oz (250 g) small eggplants, thickly sliced
Salt
$1/_4$ cup (60 ml) olive oil
2 zucchinis (courgettes), cut into chunks
1 green and 1 red bell peppers, halved, cored, deseeded and sliced into wide strips
3 ripe medium tomatoes, peeled and cut into quarters
1 tablespoon chopped fresh Italian parsley
2 teaspoons chopped fresh basil leaves
2 teaspoons chopped fresh marjoram or oregano
1 large onion, sliced
2 cloves garlic, minced
Salt and freshly-ground black pepper, to taste
Crusty bread, to serve

Serves 4–6

1 Place the eggplant slices in a colander and sprinkle liberally with salt. Set aside for 30 minutes, then rinse the eggplant slices and dry with paper towels.
2 Heat 1 tablespoon of the olive oil in a skillet until very hot and fry $1/_2$ of the eggplant slices over medium heat until just lightly browned on both sides, 1–2 minutes. Remove from the heat and transfer to a large baking pan about 2 in (5 cm) deep. Top the fried eggplant with the zucchini, bell pepper strips and tomato. Add a little more olive oil to the skillet and repeat to fry the remaining eggplant slices. Remove from the heat and spoon the fried eggplant over the prepared vegetables in the baking pan, and then sprinkle with all the herbs.
3 Preheat the oven to 350 °F (180 °C).
4 Heat the remaining olive oil in a skillet and sauté the onion over medium heat for 1–2 minutes until transparent. Add the garlic and sauté for 30 seconds. Remove from the heat, spread over the vegetables in the baking pan and sprinkle with salt and pepper to taste. Cover with foil (dull side up) and bake the vegetables in the oven for 40 minutes. Remove the foil and bake for 10 more minutes or until the vegetables are tender. Serve hot or warm with crusty bread.

Chickpea and Eggplant Stew

1 cup (200 g) dried garbanzo beans (chickpeas), soaked in water overnight in the refrigerator
1 lb (500 g) eggplants, quartered lengthwise, then sliced thickly
Salt, to taste
$1/4$ cup (60 ml) olive oil
1 medium onion, chopped
2 cloves garlic, minced
2 ripe tomatoes, peeled and chopped
$1^1/_2$ tablespoons chopped fresh Italian parsley
Freshly-ground black pepper, to taste
Pita bread, to serve

Serves 4–6

1 Drain the soaked beans and place in a saucepan. Pour in enough water to cover and bring to a boil. Cover the pan and simmer over low heat for $1^1/_2$–2 hours, until tender. Remove from the heat and drain, reserving about 1 cup (250 ml) of the cooking liquid. Return the chickpeas to the saucepan.

2 Place th eggplant pieces in a colander, sprinkle generously with salt and set aside for 30 minutes. Rinse and dry with paper towels.

3 Heat 1 tablespoon of the olive oil in a skillet and sauté the onion over medium heat until translucent, 1–2 minutes. Add the garlic and sauté for 30 seconds. Remove from the heat and add the onion mixture to the beans.

4 Heat the remaining oil in the skillet and fry the eggplant pieces over medium heat until lightly browned but not completely cooked, 2–3 minutes. Remove from the heat and spoon over the chickpeas in the pan. Add the chopped tomatoes, $1/2$ of the parsley, salt and pepper to taste. Cover and simmer over low heat, without stirring, until the eggplant is cooked, about 20 minutes. Remove from the heat.

5 Mix the eggplant gently through the chickpeas. If the mixture looks too dry, add a little chickpea liquid. Pile onto a serving platter and sprinkle with the remaining parsley. Serve hot or at room temperature with pita bread.

Fettucine with Prosciutto and Arugula

8 oz (250 g) dried or 1 lb (500 g)
  fresh fettucine
$^1/_2$ cup (125 ml) extra-virgin
  olive oil
1 medium onion, finely chopped
4 slices prosciutto, cut into thin
  strips
2 cloves garlic, finely chopped
4 tablespoons dry white wine
Salt and freshly-ground black
  pepper, to taste
8 oz (250 g) fresh arugula,
  trimmed, washed and dried well
Grated parmesan cheese, to serve
  (optional)

Serves 4

1 Bring a large saucepan of lightly salted water to a boil and cook the dried pasta according to the instructions on the packet, until just tender or *al dente*. If using fresh pasta, cook for a much shorter period. Remove from the heat, drain and keep warm.
2 Heat the olive oil in a large skillet and sauté the onion over medium heat for 1–2 minutes until transparent. Add the prosciutto and garlic and sauté for 1–2 minutes until the prosciutto turns pink. Season with the wine, salt and pepper to taste, then simmer uncovered until most of the wine has evaporated. Add the arugula and cook until just wilted, tossing often. Remove from the heat, add to the pasta and mix well. Transfer to serving platters and serve immediately with parmesan cheese if desired.

Parsley and Parmesan Bowtie Pasta

8 oz (250 g) dried farfalle

$^1/_2$ cup (125 ml) olive oil

2 cloves garlic, crushed

1 cup (40 g) fresh Italian parsley, chopped

4 tablespoons freshly-squeezed lemon juice

4 tablespoons freshly-grated parmesan cheese

Salt and freshly-ground black pepper, to taste

Serves 4

1 Bring a large saucepan of lightly salted water to a boil and cook the dried pasta according to the instructions on the packet, until just tender or *al dente*. Remove from the heat and drain.

2 Combine the olive oil, garlic and parsley in a saucepan and cook over medium heat until fragrant, 1–2 minutes. Remove from the heat, stir in the lemon juice and pour over the cooked pasta. Add the cheese, salt and pepper to taste and toss until well combined. Transfer to serving platters and serve immediately.

Note: A bit of grated lemon rind can be added to give this dish an extra tang.

Fusilli in Tomato Mozzarella and Basil Sauce

8 oz (250 g) dried mixed red, white and green fusilli

4 ripe large tomatoes, chopped

8 oz (250 g) mozzarella cheese, cubed

2 tablespoons fresh basil leaves

Salt and freshly-ground black pepper, to taste

$^1/_2$ cup (125 ml) olive oil

Serves 4

1 Bring a large saucepan of lightly salted water to a boil and cook the dried pasta according to the instructions on the packet, until just tender or *al dente*. Remove from the heat and drain.

2 Combine all the other ingredients in a large bowl and mix well. Add the pasta and toss until well coated. Transfer to serving platters and serve immediately.

Note: This dish makes a delicious salad if left to become cold.

Spaghetti with Garlic and Olive Oil

8 oz (250 g) dried or 1 lb (500 g)
  fresh spaghetti
$1/_2$ cup (125 ml) extra-virgin
  olive oil
6 cloves garlic, thinly sliced
1–2 red finger-length chili peppers,
  halved and deseeded, finely
  chopped (optional)
3 tablespoons finely-chopped
  fresh parsley
Salt and freshly-ground black
  pepper, to taste
Canned anchovy fillets, to serve
  (optional)

Toasted Breadcrumbs
3 tablespoons olive oil
4 tablespoons coarse soft white
  breadcrumbs

Serves 4

1 Prepare the Toasted Breadcrumbs first by heating the olive oil in a skillet and tossing the breadcrumbs over medium heat until golden and crisp, 1–2 minutes. Remove from the heat and set aside.

2 Bring a large saucepan of lightly salted water to a boil and cook the dried pasta according to the instructions on the packet, until just tender or *al dente*. If using fresh pasta, cook for a much shorter period. Removed from the heat and toss with 2 tablespoons of the extra virgin olive oil. Cover and set aside (it must be ready to use immediately after the next step).

3 Heat the remaining olive oil in a clean skillet and sauté the garlic and chili (if using) over medium heat until fragrant and just golden, about 30 seconds. Do not overcook. Remove from the heat and immediately pour into the pan with the spaghetti. Add the parsley, salt and pepper to taste and toss until well blended. Transfer to serving bowls, top with the anchovy fillets (if using) and serve with the Toasted Breadcrumbs on the side.

Note: This is one of the easiest pasta dishes you can make. The Toasted Breadcrumbs need not be used, but they do add interest to the pasta. The chili peppers can be omitted, but this dish is regarded as a hangover cure, and their inclusion is a must for this purpose—or if you simply like chili!

Chicken Casserole

1 fresh chicken (2 lbs/1 kg), cut into 8 pieces
1 teaspoon salt
$^1/_2$ cup (125 ml) distilled white vinegar
10 oz (300 g) okra, stalk tip trimmed
3 tablespoons olive oil
2 tablespoons butter
1 onion, diced
1 clove garlic, minced
One 14-oz (425-g) can chopped tomatoes, with liquid
2 tablespoons tomato paste
2 teaspoons sugar
$^1/_2$ cup (125 ml) water
1 bay leaf
Salt and freshly-ground black pepper, to taste
Finely-chopped fresh parsley, to serve

Serves 6

1 Rinse the chicken pieces well and dry with paper towels. Set aside.

2 In a large bowl, dissolve the salt in the vinegar. Add the okra and mix with your hands until well coated. Allow to stand for 30 minutes, then rinse the okra and drain well.

3 Heat the olive oil and butter in a large, wide saucepan and fry the chicken pieces over medium heat until evenly browned, about 5 minutes. Remove from the heat and set aside.

4 Add the onion to the pan and sauté over medium heat until transparent, 1–2 minutes. Stir in the garlic and sauté for 20 seconds. Add all the other ingredients, except the parsley, and bring to boil. Reduce the heat to low and return the fried chicken pieces to the pan, turning to coat well with the sauce. Place the okra carefully on top of the chicken pieces in the pan; they should not be covered with the sauce. Cover and simmer until tender, about 20 minutes. Remove from the heat.

5 Transfer the chicken pieces and okra to serving platters, spoon the sauce over and sprinkle with the chopped parsley. Serve hot with a pilaf.

Garlic Roast Chicken with Herbs

1 fresh roasting chicken (3 lbs/
  1$^1/_2$ kg)
Salt and freshly-ground black
  pepper, to taste
6 sprigs fresh thyme
3 sprigs fresh rosemary
2 small bay leaves
$^1/_4$ cup (60 ml) olive oil
40 large cloves garlic, unpeeled
Thick slices of French bread, to
  serve

Serves 6–8

1 Preheat the oven to 375 °F (190 °C).
2 Clean the chicken, rinse well and dry with paper
towels. Rub the inside and outside of the chicken with
salt and pepper. Place 3 sprigs thyme, 1 sprig rosemary
and 1 bay leaf in the cavity.
3 Heat the olive oil in a large skillet and fry the chicken
over medium heat for about 3 minutes on each side,
until lightly colored all over. Remove from the heat and
transfer the chicken to a deep casserole dish just large
enough to hold it. Place 2–3 cloves of garlic in the cavity, and the remainder around the chicken. Pour over
the oil from the skillet and place the remaining herb
sprigs and bay leaf on top of the chicken. Cover the
dish tightly, seal well with a strip of foil around the rim,
scrunching it to form a tight seal. Bake in the oven for
1$^1/_4$ hours—do not uncover during cooking.
4 Remove the dish from the oven and allow to stand,
covered, for 10 minutes before serving. Meanwhile,
toast the bread slices and arrange in a serving basket.
5 Serve the roast chicken, whole or carved into pieces,
with the garlic cloves and the toasted bread. Squeeze
the garlic out of its skin onto the toast or chicken.

Note: For the best effect, uncover the chicken at the
table so the full aroma is enjoyed.

Grilled Chicken with Antipasti

4 tablespoons butter

4 cloves garlic, minced

One 15-oz (425-g) can white
  kidney beans, drained and
  rinsed

4 tablespoons light cream

Salt and ground white pepper, to
  taste

1 fresh chicken (about 2 lbs/
  1 kg), cut into bite-sized pieces

3 tablespoons olive oil, mixed
  with 3 tablespoons freshly-
  squeezed lemon juice

12 slices prosciutto

6 marinated artichoke hearts,
  to serve

Pitted black olives, to serve

Roasted red bell pepper strips,
  to serve

Serves 6

1 Melt the butter in a skillet and sauté the garlic and beans over medium heat for 2–3 minutes. Remove from the heat and process to a purée in a food processor. Add the cream, salt and pepper to taste and mix well. Set aside.

2 Heat a pan grill or broiler and grill the chicken pieces over medium heat, basting with the olive oil mixture, for about 5 minutes on each side until cooked. (Alternatively bake in a preheated oven at 375 °F (190 °C) for about 20 minutes or until cooked). Remove from the heat and set aside, then grill the prosciutto slices until crisp.

3 Arrange the chicken pieces with the artichoke, olives and bell pepper strips on serving platters, then spoon on the bean purée. Top with the crispy prosciutto slices and serve immediately.

Note: Serve the juicy chicken pieces and crispy prosciutto with a selection of delicious antipasti bought from the delicatessen. Artichokes, olives and bell peppers are suggested here, but you could try marinated eggplant and mushrooms.

Tuna and Swordfish Carpaccio

5 oz (150 g) thick tuna steaks
5 oz (150 g) thick swordfish steaks
Ice cubes
Extra virgin olive oil
1 onion, halved and thinly sliced
2 tablespoons drained capers
1 tablespoon very finely-chopped
  fresh parsley
1 small red finger-length chili
  pepper, deseeded and minced
  (optional)
Radicchio (red chicory) leaves, to
  garnish
Salt and freshly-ground black
  pepper, to serve
Crusty bread

Serves 6

1 Remove the skins from the fish if present. Prepare a bowl of cold water added with ice cubes. Heat a skillet until very hot, add 2 teaspoons of olive oil and swirl the pan around to coat well. Add a fish steak and sear very briefly on each side, then hold the steak with tongs, and sear each of the narrow sides. The fish should not be browned; searing takes barely 30 seconds in all. Remove the fish from the pan and plunge immediately into the bowl of iced water to stop the cooking process. Continue to sear the remaining fish steaks in the same manner.

2 Remove the fish from the iced water and pat dry with paper towels. Wrap in plastic wrap and freeze in the freezer for 4–6 hours, or until just beginning to firm.

3 Using a sharp knife, slice the fish steaks into 1 x 2-in (3 x 5-cm) paper-thin slices. Cut any trimmings into fine shreds. On 6 serving platters, arrange alternate slices of each fish, overlapping to form a circle. Mix the fish shreds and place a pile in the center of each plate. Scatter the onion slices and capers on top. Sprinkle with the parsley and chili (if using), and drizzle about 1 tablespoon of olive oil over each portion. Garnish with radicchio leaves and serve with salt, pepper and crusty bread.

Note: The initial searing of the fish in this recipe is not traditional, but it removes any potentially harmful bacteria on the surface. If you are sure that the fish is extremely fresh, you may decide to dispense with the searing. Purchase fish steaks about 1 in ($2^1/_2$ cm) thick. Either fish can be used on its own, but the two colors of the different fish make the dish more attractive. If the prepared carpaccio is not to be served immediately, cover with plastic wrap and refrigerate until required —it should be served on the same day. An alternative serving method is to top the fish with chopped black olives and chili pepper, then drizzle with olive oil.

Marinated Squid and Octopus

$1^1/_2$ lbs (750 g) baby octopus
$1^1/_2$ lbs (750 g) squids
$1/_2$ cup (125 ml) white wine
  vinegar
$1/_2$ onion studded with 6 cloves
3 bay leaves
6 white peppercorns
1 teaspoon salt, or to taste
$1/_2$ tablespoon finely-chopped
  fresh dill
$1/_2$ cup (125 ml) olive oil
4 tablespoons freshly-squeezed
  lemon juice
Ground white pepper, to taste
Lemon wedges, to serve

Serves 6

1 Clean the octopus, removing and discarding the heads and the little hard ball or "beak" in the center of each octopus. Rinse the squids, pull out the heads and attached intestines from the tubelike bodies. Discard the heads but retaining the tentacles, and remove the beak from the mouth. Clean the body tubes, removing and discarding the long, thin cartilage.

2 In a large pot, bring 8 cups (2 liters) of water to a rolling boil. Add the vinegar, clove-studded onion, bay leaves, peppercorns and salt, and boil for about 10 minutes. Add the octopus and cook until tender, 20–30 minutes. Add the squid and simmer over medium heat for about 3 minutes. Remove the squid and octopus from the pot and refresh under cold running water. Discard the contents of the pot. Remove any skins from the seafood. Cut the octopus and squid tentacles into chunks and slice the squid bodies into thin rings.

3 Combine the seafood with the dill, olive oil and lemon juice in a large glass or ceramic bowl, and mix well. Cover and marinate overnight in the refrigerator. Sprinkle with white pepper and serve chilled with lemon wedges.

Pan-fried Fish with Red Pepper Sauce

1 lb (500 g) white fish fillets,
  rinsed and drained
$^1/_2$ cup (60 g) all-purpose (plain)
  flour, seasoned with salt and
  freshly-ground black pepper to
  taste
Olive oil, for shallow-frying
Asparagus spears, blanched, to
  serve
Lemon wedges, to serve

Red Pepper Sauce
2 Roasted Bell Peppers (page 23)
  or canned pimientos
1 clove garlic, peeled
Pinch of cayenne pepper
Salt, to taste
$^1/_4$ cup (60 ml) dry white wine
1 tablespoon olive oil

1 Roll the fish fillets in the seasoned flour until well coated. Heat the olive oil in a large skillet and fry the coated fish, in a single layer, for 2–4 minutes on each side, until the flesh flakes when tested with a fork or knife point. Remove from the heat and keep warm.
2 To make the Red Pepper Sauce, process the Roasted Bell Peppers or pimientos and garlic in a food processor until smooth. Transfer to a small saucepan, add the cayenne pepper, salt, wine and olive oil and warm over low heat for about 5 minutes, stirring occasionally. Remove from the heat.
3 Spoon the Red Pepper Sauce onto serving platters and top with the fried fish. Serve hot with asparagus spears and lemon wedges.

Serves 4

Fish Baked in Tomato Sauce

1 lb (500 g) fish steaks

Salt and ground white pepper, to taste

Chopped fresh parsley, to serve

Tomato Sauce

$1/3$ cup (100 ml) olive oil

2 onions, halved and thinly sliced

2 cloves garlic, finely chopped

$1/2$ cup (50 g) chopped celery, including leaves

$1/2$ cup (50 g) thinly-sliced carrot

$1^1/2$ cups (300 g) chopped, peeled fresh or canned tomatoes

$1/2$ cup (125 ml) water

1 Clean the fish, then drain well. Rub a little salt and pepper into both sides of the fish and set aside.

2 To prepare the Tomato Sauce, heat the oil in a skillet and sauté the onion, garlic, celery and carrot over medium heat for 2–3 minutes. Stir in the chopped tomato and water, and season with salt and pepper to taste. Cover and simmer over low heat for about 20 minutes. Remove from the heat.

3 Preheat the oven to 350 °F (180 °C).

4 Spread $1/2$ of the Tomato Sauce over the base of a baking pan and arrange the seasoned fish steaks on top. Spoon over the remaining sauce and bake in the oven for 30 minutes, or until the fish flakes easily when tested with a fork. Remove from the heat, sprinkle with chopped parsley and serve hot or cold.

Serves 4

Grilled Swordfish Skewers

1 lb (500 g) swordfish fillets
Bamboo skewers, soaked in water
for 1 hour before using

Marinade
$1/4$ cup (60 ml) freshly-squeezed
lemon juice
2 tablespoons olive oil
1 small onion, sliced
1 teaspoon paprika
1 teaspoon salt
$1/2$ teaspoon freshly-ground black
pepper
2 bay leaves, crumbled

Lemon Sauce (Limon Salçası)
$1/4$ cup (60 ml) olive oil
$1/4$ cup (60 ml) freshly-squeezed
lemon juice
$1/4$ cup (10 g) finely-chopped
fresh Italian parsley
Salt and freshly-ground black
pepper, to taste

1 When purchasing swordfish, ask for 1- in (3-cm) thick fillets. Remove the skin if present and rinse well, then cut into 1-in (3-cm) cubes.

2 Combine the Marinade ingredients in a bowl. Add the fish cubes, turning to coat well with the Marinade. Cover and refrigerate for 1–2 hours, turning occasionally.

3 To make the Lemon Sauce, combine all the ingredients in a screwtop jar, seal tightly and then shake until well blended.

4 Thread the fish cubes onto bamboo skewers and grill on a pan grill or over glowing charcoal for about 10 minutes until cooked, basting with the Marinade and turning frequently. Serve hot with dipping bowls of the Lemon Sauce and a pilaf if desired.

Note: Lemon Sauce (Limon Salçası) is a suitable dressing for grilled, fried, boiled and baked fish, salads and vegetables.

Serves 4

Spiced Shrimp

1 lb (500 g) fresh medium shrimp, peeled and deveined, tails intact
$1/_2$ teaspoon salt
$1/_3$ cup (100 ml) olive oil
4 cloves garlic, finely chopped
1 tablespoon chopped red finger-length chili pepper
1 teaspoon ground cumin
1 teaspoon ground ginger
1 teaspoon ground turmeric
$1^1/_2$ teaspoons paprika
$1/_4$ cup (60 ml) water
3 tablespoons finely-chopped fresh coriander leaves (cilantro)
Lemon wedges, to serve
Crusty bread, to serve

1 Place the shrimp in a colander, sprinkle with the salt and toss through. Set aside.

2 Heat the oil in a large skillet and sauté the garlic, chili and spices over medium heat until fragrant, about 1 minute. Add the seasoned shrimp, increase the heat to high and toss until just pink, 1–2 minutes. Pour in the water and simmer uncovered until the sauce has been absorbed. Stir in the chopped coriander, toss well and remove from the heat. Serve immediately with lemon wedges and crusty bread.

Serves 4

Grilled Seafood with Romesco Sauce

1 lb (500 g) squids (calamari) or
  baby octopus
Olive oil
1 clove garlic, finely chopped
1 lb (500 g) fresh large shrimp
1 teaspoon coarse salt
1 lb (500 g) fresh clams, scrubbed
  clean
1 lb (500 g) fresh mussels,
  scrubbed clean

Romesco Sauce
$1/_3$ cup (100 ml) olive oil
1 medium onion, quartered
2 cloves garlic, peeled
1–2 red finger-length chili peppers,
  deseeded
3 ripe medium tomatoes, peeled
  and deseeded, or one 15-oz
  (425-g) can chopped tomatoes
$1/_4$ cup (60 ml) water
$1/_4$ cup (60 ml) dry white wine
$1/_2$ cup (75 g) whole blanched
  almonds, toasted
1 Roasted Red Bell Pepper
  (page 23) or 1 canned pimiento
1 tablespoon red wine vinegar
Salt and freshly-ground black
  pepper, to taste

1 Clean the squids or octopus as instructed on page 76, then place in a large bowl with 2 tablespoons olive oil and the garlic. Mix well and set aside for at least 20 minutes. In another bowl, sprinkle the shrimp with the salt and toss through.

2 To make the Romesco Sauce, heat 1 tablespoon of the olive oil in a saucepan and sauté the onion, garlic and chili pepper over medium heat until soft, 1–2 minutes. Stir in the tomatoes, water and wine and bring to a boil, then cover and simmer over low heat for 30 minutes. Remove from the heat and allow to cool.

3 Process the almonds in a food processor until fine. Add the tomato mixture and Roasted Bell Pepper or pimiento, and process to a purée. With the motor running, gradually pour in the remaining olive oil and vinegar. Add salt and pepper to taste and continue to process until the mixture has the consistency of a thick sauce. Transfer to a serving bowl.

4 Heat a barbecue hot plate or large skillet until hot and cook all the seafood over medium heat, tossing and constantly basting with olive oil, until just cooked, 3–5 minutes. The shrimp should be just pink and the clams and mussels must be removed from the pan when they have just opened. Serve the seafood immediately with the bowl of Romesco Sauce on the side.

Serves 6

Lamb and Vegetable Kebabs

1 lb (500 g) boneless lamb leg meat, cubed

16 small whole onions, peeled

1 red and 1 green bell pepper, cored, deseed and sliced into pieces the size of the onion

8 bamboo skewers, soaked in water for 1 hour before using

Marinade

Freshly-squeezed juice of 1 lemon

$1/4$ cup (60 ml) olive oil

1 onion, thinly sliced

1 bay leaf, crumbled

$1/2$ teaspoon dried thyme

$1/2$ teaspoon freshly-ground black pepper

1 teaspoon salt

Serves 4

1 In a large bowl, combine the Marinade ingredients, except the salt, and mix well. Add the lamb cubes and mix until well coated. Cover and marinate in the refrigerator for 4–6 hours, turning occasionally. Leave for longer if desired. Stir in the salt just before cooking.

2 Bring a saucepan of lightly salted water to a boil and boil the onion for about 5 minutes. Remove from the heat and drain.

3 Thread the lamb cubes onto bamboo skewers, alternating with whole onions and bell pepper pieces. Grill the skewers on a pan grill or over glowing charcoal for about 10 minutes until cooked, basting with the Marinade and turning frequently. After sealing the meat, move the skewers to the cooler part of the grill or raise the grid, otherwise the vegetables will burn. Serve hot with a pilaf.

Roast Lamb with Rosemary

2 racks of lamb (3–4 ribs each, depending on the size of racks), fat trimmed
1 slice pancetta or streaky bacon
3 sprigs fresh rosemary
3 cloves garlic
Salt and freshly-ground black pepper, to taste
3 tablespoons olive oil
Fresh rosemary sprigs, to garnish

Serves 6–8

1 Preheat the oven to 375 °F (190 °C).
2 Using a sharp knife, make several incisions in the outer surface of each rack. Slice the pancetta or bacon into short strips, pull the leaves from 1 sprig rosemary, and thinly slice 2 cloves garlic. Insert a pancetta strip, a few rosemary leaves and a slice of garlic into each incision. Season the lamb with salt and pepper to taste, and brush all over with a little olive oil.
3 Place the remaining rosemary sprigs and garlic clove in the base of a roasting pan and pour in the remaining olive oil. Place the lamb racks over the rosemary, meat side up. Roast for 40–50 minutes, until the lamb is tender and pink inside, basting occasionally with the oil in the pan. Transfer the lamb to a serving platter, cover loosely with foil, and allow to stand for 5 minutes before serving. Garnish with rosemary sprigs.

Ground Meat Kebabs

This is a street food in Maghreb, served in bread with an extra sprinkling of salt and cumin, but I like to add salad vegetables. Purchase meat that is not too lean. If you are using long skewers, have two portions of meat mixture on each skewer. Use one portion on short skewers. To cook the kebabs, remove the grid from the barbecue if possible and place skewers so that the ends rest on the sides of the barbecue. A Habachi barbecue is ideal for cooking these.

1 small onion, quartered
2 tablespoons fresh Italian parsley leaves
1 tablespoon fresh coriander leaves (cilantro)
1 teaspoon paprika
$1/2$ teaspoon ground allspice
$1/4$ teaspoon cayenne pepper
$1/2$ teaspoon ground cumin
1 teaspoon salt
$1/2$ teaspoon freshly-ground black pepper, to taste
1 lb (500 g) ground lamb or beef
Olive oil, for brushing
Pita or other flat bread, warmed, to serve

1 Process the onion, parsley and coriander leaves in a food processor until smooth. Transfer to a mixing bowl, combine with the spices, salt and pepper and mix well, then add the ground meat and mix until well blended. Cover and refrigerate for 30 minutes.

2 Wet your hands, take about 2 heaping tablespoons of the meat mixture and shape it into a 3-in (10-cm) cylinder, then thread onto a barbecue skewer, pressing hard to wrap the meat mixture around the skewer. Continue to make the kebabs in the same manner with the remaining meat mixture. Place the skewers in a tray, cover and refrigerate for 1 hour.

3 Preheat a barbecue grill. Lightly brush the kebabs with olive oil and grill until cooked through, 6–8 minutes, turning frequently. (Alternatively, grill on a pan grill or under a broiler for the same period or longer without threading onto the skewers.) Remove from the heat, slide the kebabs off the skewers and serve with warm bread.

Makes about 20

Beef Provençal

1 lb (500 g) lean stewing beef, fat
  trimmed and cubed
1 carrot, cut into chunks
1 tablespoon olive oil
3 slices lean bacon, diced
1 onion, cut into wedges
2 cloves garlic, crushed
1/2 cup (125 ml) water
1 strip orange rind
Salt and freshly-ground black
  pepper, to taste

Marinade
1 onion, sliced
Bouquet garni (2 sprigs each
  thyme and parsley and 1 bay
  leaf, tied together)
1/2 cup (125 ml) red wine
1 tablespoon brandy

Serves 4

1 Combine the Marinade ingredients in a large plastic container and mix well. Add the beef cubes and carrot chunks and mix until well coated. Cover and refrigerate for 6 hours or overnight, shaking the container occasionally. Remove the beef and flavoring ingredients from the container and place in a large casserole. Reserve the Marinade liquid.

2 Preheat the oven to 350 °F (180 °C).

3 Heat the olive oil in a skillet and sauté the bacon over medium heat until lightly browned, 1–2 minutes. Add the onion wedges and sauté until tinged with brown flecks. Add the garlic and sauté for 30 seconds. Pour in the reserved Marinade liquid and water, add the orange rind, salt and pepper to taste, and bring to a boil. Remove from the heat, pour over the beef in the casserole.

4 Cover the casserole and bake in the oven for about 2 hours, or until the beef is tender—check after 1 hour that there is sufficient liquid to cover, and add water and adjust the seasonings if necessary. Serve hot.

Note: Boneless shin of beef or chuck steak is ideal for this daube, but other stewing beef can also be used. The orange rind adds an extra flavor; dried is preferred, but a piece of fresh rind, removed in a wide strip with a swivel peeler, can be used instead.

Complete List of Recipes

Appetizers
Baked Ricotta Cheese with
   Olives and Sundried
   Tomatoes   35
Bruschetta with Arugula   24
Deep-fried Calamari
   Rings   27
Garlic Mushrooms   37
Herbal Toasts with Bean
   Dip   33
Homemade Anchovy
   Paste   33
Marinated Eggplant   22
Marinated Olives   20–21
Olive Tapenade   19
Onion and Olive Tart   28
Roasted Bell Peppers   23
Stuffed Red Peppers   37
Turkish Pita Bread   31

Basics and Sauces
Basic Italian Dressing   13
Classic Italian Tomato Sauce
   17
Classic Oil and Lemon
   Dressing   13
Classic Oil and Vinegar
   Dressing   13
Homemade Mayonnaise   18
Homemade Pesto Sauce   15
Spanish Tomato Sauce   17

Meat
Beef Provençal   94

Ground Meat Kebabs   93
Lamb and Vegetable
   Kebabs   88
Roast Lamb with
   Rosemary   90

Pasta
Fettucine with Prosciutto
   and Arugula   63
Fusilli in Tomato Mozzarella
   and Basil Sauce   64
Parsley and Parmesan
   Bowtie Pasta   64
Spaghetti with Garlic and
   Olive Oil   66

Poultry
Chicken Casserole   68
Garlic Roast Chicken with
   Herbs   71
Grilled Chicken with
   Antipasti   73

Salads
Beet Salad with Oranges
   and Walnuts   45
Borlotti Bean and Radicchio
   Salad   45
Cherry Tomato, Bocconcini
   and Basil Skewers   39
Orange and Carrot Salad   46
Orange and Olive Salad   41
Roasted tomato and Bell
   Pepper Salad   41

Tomato and Olive Salad   39
Tomato, Onion and Lemon
   Salad   42

Seafood
Fish Baked in Tomato sauce
   81
Grilled Seafood with
   Romesco Sauce   86
Grilled Swordfish
   Skewers   83
Marinated Squid and
   Octopus   77
Pan-fried Fish with Red
   Pepper Sauce   78
Spiced Shrimp   84
Tuna and Swordfish
   Carpaccio   75

Soups
Broccoli Soup with Potato
   51
Chickpea Soup with
   Linguine   52
Garlic Almond Soup   51
Gaspacho   48

Vegetables
Chickpea and Eggplant
   Stew   60
Mixed Vegetable
   Ratatouille   59
Stuffed Tomatoes   54
Stuffed Vine Leaves   57